Ideas IN ART

Rosemary Etherton

Contents

Ideas IN ART

The paper sits in front of you. It is blank. The clay sits on the table. It is a blob with no shape. What are you going to **create**?

Where do artists get their ideas? Let's look at some **famous** artworks from around the world. Let's take a look at the ideas in art.

Idea:
A BUSHRANGER

Ned Kelly, 1946 – Sidney Nolan,
National Gallery of Australia, Canberra

Who is on that horse? It's Ned Kelly, Australia's most famous **bushranger**. Where is he going? Far, far away so the police can't catch him.

Ned Kelly lived over 100 years ago. This artist loved painting stories from Ned Kelly's life.

Artist File

Who:	Sidney Nolan, an Australian artist
Born:	1917 and died in 1992
Fact:	Sidney Nolan made 27 paintings about Ned Kelly.

Art Hunt

Look at the trees in the painting. How did the artist make them look a long way away?

Idea: MACHINES

Propellers, 1918 – Fernand Léger, Museum of Modern Art, New York

Look at the different shapes and patterns in this painting. What is this machine? Do the pipes go up? Do the wheels go round?

This artist liked machines. He painted many of them. He made his machines look exciting and fun.

Artist File

Who:	Fernand Léger, a French artist
Born:	1881 and died in 1955
Fact:	Fernand Léger also made **sculptures** and films.

Art Hunt

How many circles, rectangles, cylinders and squares can you find in this painting?

Idea:
EVERYDAY LIFE

The girls at school, 1959 – John Brack, Private collection

This artist liked to paint his daughters. Here they are in their school uniforms, with their hair neatly tied back in bows. They are carrying flowers, but they look a bit worried. Perhaps they have heard the bell!

Artist File

Who:	John Brack, an Australian artist
Born:	1920 and died in 1999
Fact:	John Brack liked to paint the people he saw around him.

Art Hunt

Look how carefully the artist painted the checked school uniforms. They stand out from the dark, solid bricks behind the girls.

Idea: **MUSIC**

Empress of the Blues, 1974 – Romare Beardon, Smithsonian American Art Museum

This artist loved jazz music. He made many artworks of his friends playing music. This artwork shows people playing and moving to the loud jazz music. The painting makes us feel like we want to dance and listen to music, too!

Artist File

Who:	Romare Beardon, an American artist
Born:	1911 and died in 1988
Fact:	Romare Beardon also drew cartoons.

Art Hunt

How many musicians can you count? What instruments are they playing?

Idea:
SCARY STORIES

Maman, 1999 –
Louise Bourgeois,
National Gallery
of Canada

Cold, dark skin and tall, skinny legs – watch out! There is a giant spider here! Just think what life would be like if this big spider was real.

This artist was thinking of scary children's stories when she made this spider.

Artist File

Who:	Louise Bourgeois, a French artist
Born:	1911 and died in 2010
Fact:	Louise Bourgeois makes her artworks from wood, stone and **bronze**.

Art Hunt

This is a spider. How many legs does this artwork have?

Idea: **PEOPLE**

Two old men disputing, c. 1628 – Rembrandt, National Gallery of Victoria

This artist looked at people to get ideas. He used faces to show feelings. The men look wise and are talking about something. The light comes from a window we cannot see. The light shows us which man is talking in the painting.

Artist File

Who:	Rembrandt, a Dutch artist
Born:	1606 and died in 1669
Fact:	Rembrandt was an art teacher, too.

Art Hunt

Look at the old man's eyes.
Can you see the tears?

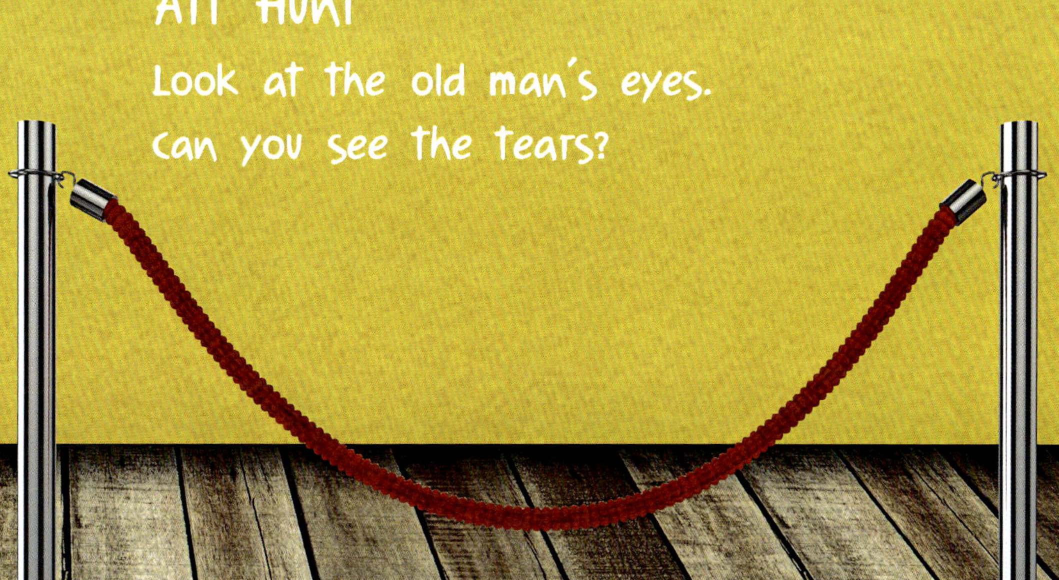

Idea: PETS

This artwork is of the artist's pet owl. A friend found the owl and gave it to the artist. The artist looked after the owl for many years.

Owls have big eyes. Look at the shapes the artist has used to make its face.

Artist File

Who:	Pablo Picasso, a Spanish artist
Born:	1881 and died in 1973
Fact:	Picasso made thousands and thousands of pieces of artwork!

Art Hunt

What do you think the black lines on the owl show?

Idea: FEELINGS

Blue Poles, 1952 – Jackson Pollock, National Gallery of Australia, Canberra

Drip! Flick, splash and **pour!** This artist wanted to find new ways to paint. So he did not just use brushes for this painting. He also dripped and flicked paint onto it.

He also wanted to show how some things made him feel. He used those feelings to make his art.

Artist File

Who:	Jackson Pollock, an American artist
Born:	1912 and died in 1956
Fact:	Jackson Pollock put his paintings on the floor to paint.

Art Hunt

Why do you think this painting is called Blue Poles?

Idea: **HOME**

Napperby death spirit Dreaming, 1980 – Tim Leura Tjapaltjarri and Clifford Possum Tjapaltjarri, National Gallery of Victoria

Pretend this painting is on the floor. You need to look down on the painting. The artists have made the painting as if they are looking down at their land from the sky.

The artists have used thousands of dots to create this painting.

Art Hunt

There are hunting men with spears sitting around three campfires. Can you find them?

Artist File

Who: Tim Leura Tjapaltjarri and Clifford Possum Tjapaltjarri, an Australian artist

Born: Tim was born around 1929 and died in 1984. Clifford was born around 1932 and died in 2002

Fact: These two artists were brothers. They painted this painting together.

Idea:

THE OCEAN

The Great Wave off Kanagawa, 1832 – Katsushika Hokusai, The Metropolitan Museum of Art

Row hard, everyone! Here comes a big wave! This painting shows three fishing boats. They are being rowed by three teams of fishermen.

Look at the boats dive through the big waves. The fishermen have lots of fish to take back to shore.

Artist File

Who:	Katsushika Hokusai, a Japanese artist
Born:	1760 and died in 1849
Fact:	This artist used wood blocks to make his prints.

Art Hunt

Can you see a mountain in the distance? This is Mt Fuji.

Idea: **COLOURS**

The Bedroom, 1888 – Vincent Van Gogh, Van Gogh Museum, Amsterdam

This artist used a lot of colour in his paintings. He used bright colours in this painting of his bedroom. Bright colours made him feel at rest. The bed and the chair are painted yellow, like fresh butter.

Artist File

Who:	Vincent Van Gogh, a Dutch artist
Born:	1853 and died in 1890
Fact:	Vincent Van Gogh's paintings are famous for their strong colours.

Art Hunt

In this painting, can you see some of the artist's other paintings hanging on the wall?

Idea: **FACES**

Zappo head, 1987 – Howard Arkley, Bendigo Art Gallery, Victoria

Look at this face! The artist used a mask to create this artwork. Some people think this head looks like a very old mask. Other people think it looks like an alien's head. What do you think?

The artist used a special **airbrush** to paint this painting. This is why it looks fuzzy.

Who:	Howard Arkley, an Australian artist
Born:	1951 and died in 1999
Fact:	This artist also did paintings of houses in very bright colours.

Art Hunt

How many circles and triangles can you find in this painting?

YOU TRY IT!

It's your turn now. Here are some ideas to get you started.

Draw an Animal

Remember the artist who painted the owl? Use pencils and draw your pet or favourite animal. Use lines and patterns on your animal.

Paint Your Place

Remember the artist who painted his bedroom? Do a painting of your bedroom. Use colours to show your feelings.

You and YOUR IDEAS

So now you know some of the ways artists get ideas. Where will you get your next idea?

Perhaps you will start with a favourite story. Perhaps you will watch people and paint what you see.

Who knows where your ideas will take you...

GLOSSARY

airbrush a machine that uses air to spray paint onto the paper or canvas

ancestors people from whom you are descended, or come from

bronze a type of metal

bushranger an outlaw from long ago who hid in the bush

create to make

famous well-known; known by many people

sculptures pieces of art that are sometimes made by carving materials such as wood or stone